Be a
Circle
Maker

Be a Circle Maker

The Solution to 10,000 Problems

Mark Batterson

ZONDERVAN®

ZONDERVAN.com/
AUTHORTRACKER
follow your favorite authors

ZONDERVAN

Be a Circle Maker
Copyright © 2011 by Mark Batterson

Requests for information should be addressed to:

Zondervan, *Grand Rapids, Michigan* 49530

ISBN 978-0-310-33635-8

Published in association with the literary agency of Fedd & Company, Inc., Post Office Box 341973, Austin, TX 78734.

Cover design: *Extra Credit Projects*
Interior illustration: *iStockPhoto®*
Interior design: *Beth Shagene*

Printed in the United States of America

17 18 /CHG/ 10 9 8 7

Contents

Chapter 1

The Legend
of the Circle Maker

Young children danced in the downpour like it was the first rainfall they'd ever seen. And it was. Parents threw back their heads, opened their mouths, and caught raindrops like they were libations. And they were. When it hasn't rained in more than a year, raindrops are like diamonds falling from the sky.

It would be forever remembered as *the day*. The day thunderclaps applauded the Almighty. The day puddle jumping became an act of praise. The day the legend of the circle maker was born.

It was the first century BC, and a devastating drought threatened to destroy a generation — the generation before Jesus. The last of the Jewish prophets had died off nearly four centuries before. Miracles were such a distant memory that they seemed like a false memory. And God was nowhere to be heard. But there was one man, an eccentric sage who lived outside the walls of Jerusalem, who dared to pray anyway. His name was Honi. And even if the people could no longer hear God, he believed that God could still hear them.

When rain is plentiful, it's an afterthought. During a drought, it's the only thought. And Honi was their only hope. Famous for his ability to pray for rain, it was on this day, *the day*, that Honi would earn his moniker.

With a six-foot staff in his hand, Honi

began to turn like a math compass. His circular movement was rhythmical and methodical. Ninety degrees. One hundred eighty degrees. Two hundred seventy degrees. Three hundred sixty degrees. He never looked up as the crowd looked on. After what seemed like hours but had only been seconds, Honi stood inside the circle he had drawn. Then he dropped to his knees and raised his hands to heaven. With the authority of the prophet Elijah, who called down fire from heaven, Honi called down rain:

"Lord of the universe, I swear before Your great name that I will not move from this circle until You have shown mercy upon Your children."

The words sent a shudder down the spines of all who were within earshot that day. It wasn't just the volume of his voice; it was the authority of his tone. Not a hint of doubt. This prayer didn't originate in the vocal chords. Like water from an artesian well, the words flowed from the depth of his soul. His prayer was resolute yet humble, confident yet meek, expectant yet unassuming.

Then it happened.

As his prayer ascended to the heavens, raindrops descended to the earth. An audible gasp swept across the thousands of congregants who had encircled Honi. Every head turned heavenward as the first raindrops parachuted from the sky, but Honi's head remained bowed. The people rejoiced over each drop, but Honi wasn't satisfied with a sprinkle. Still kneeling within the circle, Honi lifted his voice over the sounds of celebration:

"Not for such *rain have I prayed, but for rain that will fill cisterns, pits, and caverns."*

The sprinkle turned into such a torrential downpour that eyewitnesses said no raindrop was smaller than an egg in size. It rained so heavily and so steadily that the people fled to the Temple Mount to escape the flash floods. Honi stayed and prayed inside his protracted circle. Once more he refined his bold request:

"Not for such rain have I prayed, but for rain of Your favor, blessing, and graciousness."

Then, like a well-proportioned sun shower on a hot and humid August afternoon, it began to rain calmly, peacefully. Each raindrop was a tangible token of God's grace. And they didn't just soak the skin; they soaked the spirit with faith. It had been difficult to believe the day before *the day*. The day after *the day*, it was impossible *not* to believe.

Eventually, the dirt turned into mud and back into dirt again. After quenching their thirst, the crowd dispersed.

And the rainmaker returned to his humble hovel on the outskirts of Jerusalem. Life returned to normal, but the legend of the circle maker had been born.

Honi was celebrated as a hometown hero by the people whose lives he had saved. But some within the Sanhedrin called the circle maker into question. A faction believed that drawing a circle and demanding rain dishonored God. Maybe it was those same members of the Sanhedrin who would criticize Jesus for healing a man's shriveled hand on the Sabbath a generation later. They threatened Honi with excommunication, but because the miracle could not be repudiated, Honi was ultimately honored for his act of prayerful bravado.

The prayer that saved a generation was deemed one of the most significant prayers in the history of Israel. The circle he drew in the sand became a sacred symbol. And the legend of Honi the circle maker stands forever as a testament to the power of a single prayer to change the course of history.

Chapter 2

Circle Makers

The earth has circled the sun more than two thousand times since *the day* Honi drew his circle in the sand, but God is still looking for circle makers. And the timeless truth secreted within this ancient legend is as true now as it was then: *Bold prayers honor God*, and *God honors bold prayers*. God isn't offended by your biggest dreams or boldest prayers. He is offended by anything less. If your prayers aren't impossible to you, they are insulting to God.

Why? Because they don't require divine intervention. But ask God to part the Red Sea or make the sun stand still or float an iron axhead, and God is moved to omnipotent action.

There is nothing God loves more than keeping promises, answering prayers, performing miracles, and fulfilling dreams. That is *who* He is. That is *what* He does. And the bigger the circle we draw, the better, because God gets more glory. The greatest moments in life are the miraculous moments when human impotence and divine omnipotence intersect — and they intersect when we draw a circle around the impossible situations in our lives and invite God to intervene.

I promise you this: God is ready and waiting. So while I have no idea what circumstances you find yourself in, I'm confident that you are only one prayer away from a dream fulfilled, a promise kept, or a miracle performed.

It is absolutely imperative at the outset that you come to terms with this simple yet life-changing truth: *God is for you.* If you don't believe that, then you'll pray small timid prayers; if you do believe it, then you'll pray big audacious prayers. And one way or another, your small timid prayers or big audacious prayers will change the trajectory of your life and turn you into two totally different people. Prayers are prophecies. They are the best predictors of your spiritual future. *Who you become* is determined by *how you pray*. Ultimately, the transcript of your prayers becomes the script of your life.

Do you want to be inspired to dream big, pray hard, and think long? Do you want to learn how to claim God-given promises, pursue God-sized dreams, and seize God-ordained opportunities — to draw prayer circles around your family, your job, your problems, and your goals? Before you learn *how* to draw prayer circles, it's important to understand *why* it is so important. Drawing prayer circles isn't some magic trick to get what you want from God. God is not a genie in a bottle, and your wish is not His command. His command better be your wish. If it's not, you won't be drawing prayer circles; you'll end up walking in circles.

Drawing prayer circles starts with discerning what God wants, what God wills. And until His sovereign will becomes your sanctified wish, your prayer life will be unplugged from its power supply. Sure, you can apply some of the principles of becoming a circle maker, and they may help you get what you want, but getting what you want isn't the goal; the goal is glorifying God by drawing circles around the promises, miracles, and dreams He wants for you.

My First Circle

Over the years, I've drawn prayer circles around promises in Scripture and promises the Holy Spirit has conceived in my spirit. I've drawn prayer circles around impossible situations and impossible people. I've drawn prayer circles around everything from life goals to pieces of property. But let me begin at the beginning and retrace the first prayer circle I ever drew.

When I was a twenty-two-year-old seminary student, I tried to plant a church on the north shore of Chicago, but that plant never took root. Six months later, with a failed church plant on my résumé, Lora and I moved from Chicago to Washington, D.C. The opportunity to attempt another church plant presented itself, and my knee-jerk reaction was to say no, but God gave me the courage to face my fears, swallow my pride, and try again.

There was nothing easy about our first year of church planting. Our total church income was $2,000 a month, and $1,600 of that went to rent the D.C. public school cafetorium where we held Sunday services. On a good Sunday, twenty-five people would show up. That's when I learned to close my eyes in worship because it was too depressing to open them. While I had a seminary education, I really had no idea how to lead. That's challenging when you *are* the leader. I felt underqualified and overwhelmed, but that is when God has you right where He wants you. That is how you learn to live in raw dependence — and raw dependence is the raw material out of which God performs His greatest miracles.

One day, as I was dreaming about the church God wanted to establish on Capitol Hill, I felt prompted by the Holy Spirit to do a prayer walk. I would often pace and pray in the spare bedroom in our house that doubled as the church office, but this prompting was different. I was reading through the book of Joshua at the time, and one of the promises jumped off the page and into my spirit.

"I'm giving you every square inch of the land you set your foot on — just as I promised Moses."

As I read that promise given to Joshua, I felt that God wanted me to stake claim to the land He had called us to and pray a perimeter all the way around Capitol Hill. I had a Honi-like confidence that just as this promise had been transferred from Moses to Joshua, God would transfer the promise to me if I had enough faith to circle it. So one hot and humid

August morning, I drew what would be my first prayer circle. It still ranks as the longest prayer walk I've ever done and the biggest prayer circle I've ever drawn.

Starting at the front door of our row house on Capitol Hill, I walked east on F Street and turned south on 8th Street. I crossed East Capitol, the street that bisects the NE and SE quadrants of the city, and turned west on M Street SE. I then completed the circle, which was actually more of a square, by heading north on South Capitol Street. I paused to pray in front of the Capitol for a few minutes. Then I completed the 4.7-mile circle by taking a right turn at Union Station and heading home.

It's hard to describe what I felt when I finished drawing that circle. My feet were sore, but my spirit soared. I felt the same kind of holy confidence the Israelites must have felt when they crossed the Jordan River on dry ground and stepped foot in the Promised Land for the first time. I couldn't wait to see the way God would honor that prayer. That prayer circle had taken nearly three hours to complete because my prayer pace is slower than my normal pace, but God has been answering that three-hour prayer for the past fifteen years.

Since *the day* I drew that prayer circle around Capitol Hill, National Community Church has grown into one church with seven locations around the metro D.C. area. We're on the verge of launching our first international campus in Berlin, Germany. And God has given us the privilege of influencing tens of thousands of people over the last decade and a half.

All Bets Are Off

As I look over my shoulder, I'm grateful for the miracles God has done, and

I'm keenly aware of the fact that every miracle has a genealogy. If you trace those miracles all the way back to their origin, you'll find a prayer circle. Miracles are the by-product of prayers that were prayed *by you* or *for you*. And that should be all the motivation you need to pray.

God has determined that certain expressions of His power will only be exercised in response to prayer. Simply put, God won't do it unless you pray for it. We have not because we ask not, or maybe I should say, we have not because we circle not. The greatest tragedy in life is the prayers that go unanswered because they go unasked.

Now here's the good news: If you do pray, all bets are off. You can live with holy anticipation because you never know how or when or where God is going to answer, but I promise you this: He will answer. And His answers are not limited by your requests. We pray out of our ignorance, but God answers out of His omniscience. We pray out of our impotence, but God answers out of His omnipotence. God has the ability to answer the prayers we should have prayed but lacked the knowledge or ability to even ask.

During my prayer walk around Capitol Hill, I drew circles around things I didn't even know how to ask for. Without even knowing it, I drew prayer circles around people who would one day come to faith in Jesus Christ at our coffeehouse on Capitol Hill that wasn't even an idea yet. Without even knowing it, I walked right by a piece of property at 8th Street and Virginia Avenue SE that we would purchase thirteen years later as a result of a $3 million gift that wasn't even a prayer yet. Without even knowing it, I walked right under a theater marquee on Barracks Row, the main street of Capitol Hill, that we would renovate and reopen as our seventh location fifteen years later.

Those answers are a testament to the power of God and a reminder that if you draw prayer circles, God will answer those prayers somehow, someway, sometime. God has been answering that prayer for fifteen years, and He'll keep answering it forever. Like Honi, your prayers have the potential to change the course of history. It's time to start circling.

Chapter 3

The Solution to Ten Thousand Problems

Imagine more than a million birds flying in formation. Now imagine them falling from the sky. There wasn't a food source within a week's walk, but God delivered dinner right to the doorstep of the Israelites while they wandered in the wilderness. Right before that quail miracle, God asks Moses a question. It's more than *a* question; it's *the* question. Your answer to this question, *the question*, will determine the size of your prayer circles.

"Is there a limit to my power?"

The obvious answer to that question is no. God is omnipotent, which means by definition, there is nothing God cannot do. Yet many of us pray as if our problems are bigger than God. So let me remind you of this high-octane truth that should fuel your faith: God is infinitely bigger than your biggest problem or biggest dream. And while we're on the topic, His grace is infinitely bigger than your biggest sin.

The modern mystic A. W. Tozer believed that a low view of God is the cause of a hundred lesser evils, but a high view of God is the solution to ten thousand temporal problems. If that's true, and I believe it is, then your biggest problem isn't an impending divorce or failing business or doctor's diagnosis. Please understand, I'm not making light of your relational or financial or health issues. I certainly don't want to minimize the overwhelming challenges you may be facing. But in order to regain a godly perspective on your problems, you have to answer this question: Are your problems bigger than God, or is God bigger than your problems? Our biggest problem is our small view of God. That is the cause of all lesser evils. And it's a high view of God that is the solution to all other problems.

Is there a limit to my power?

Have you answered *the question*? There are only two options: yes or no. Until you come to the conviction that God's grace and power know no limits, you will draw small prayer circles. Once you embrace the omnipotence of God, you'll draw ever-enlarging circles around your God-given, God-sized dreams.

How big is your God? Is He big enough to heal your marriage or heal your child? Is He bigger than a positive MRI or a negative evaluation? Is He bigger than your secret sin or secret dream?

Sizing Up God

Moses was perplexed that God could promise to provide meat for the Israelites not just for a day or a week, but for a month. It didn't add up! But at that critical juncture, when Moses had to decide whether or not to circle the promise, God posed *the question*.

Is there a limit to my power?

When God prompted me to pray for a $2 million miracle, I had to answer *the question*. It seemed like an impossible promise to me, but to the God who can provide 105 million quail out of nowhere, what's $2 million?

The size of prayers depends on the size of our God. And if God knows no limits, then neither should our prayers. God exists outside of the four space-time dimensions He created. We should pray that way!

It reminds me of the man who was

sizing up God by asking, "God, how long is a million years to you?" God said, "A million years is like a second." Then the man asked, "How much is a million dollars to you?" God said, "A million dollars is like a penny." The man smiled and said, "Could you spare a penny?" God smiled back and said, "Sure, just wait a second."

With God, there is no big or small, easy or difficult, possible or impossible. This is difficult to comprehend because all we've ever known are the four dimensions we were born into, but God is not subject to the natural laws He instituted. He has no beginning and no end. To the infinite, all finites are equal. Even our hardest prayers are easy for the Omnipotent One to answer because there is no degree of difficulty.

If you're like me, you tend to use bigger words for bigger requests. You pull out your best vocabulary words for your biggest prayers, as if God's answer depends on the correct combination of words. Trust me, it doesn't matter how long or how loud you pray; it comes down to your answer to *the question*.

Is there a limit to my power?

With God, it's never an issue of "Can He?" It's only a question of "Will He?" And while you don't always know if He *will*, you know He *can*. And because you know He can, you can pray with holy confidence.

Warts

I answered *the question* when I was thirteen years old, or maybe I should say, *the question* was answered for me. Our family visited a new church one Sunday, and a prayer team from that church showed up unannounced at our front door on Monday. The doorbell caught us a little off guard. So did their faith. After introducing themselves, they simply asked if we needed prayer for anything. At that point in my life, I struggled with severe asthma. I was hospitalized half a dozen times during my preteen years. So we asked them to ask God to heal me. That prayer team formed a prayer circle around me and laid their hands on my head. It made me feel a little uncomfortable, but I had never heard anyone pray with that much intensity. They prayed as if they believed. Then they left.

Sometime between falling asleep that night and waking up the next morning, God did a miracle, but it wasn't the miracle I expected. God answered that prayer, but it wasn't the answer I anticipated. I still had asthma the next morning, but every wart on my feet was gone. No kidding. At first I wondered if God misinterpreted the prayer. Or maybe this was some kind of prayer joke? I couldn't help but wonder if prayer was like the game of telephone where a message gets passed from person to person until it finally gets to God. Maybe somewhere between here and heaven, asthma got translated into warts. Or maybe there was someone with warts who was breathing great that day because they got my answer while I got theirs.

That's when I heard the still small voice of the Holy Spirit for the first time in my life. Please understand that Spirit-whispers are few and far between, but those whispers echo forever. The Spirit said to my spirit, *Mark, I just want you to know that I'm able.*

Like the day after *the day* that God sent rain in answer to Honi's prayer, it was hard *not* to believe the next day. Once you experience a miracle, there is no turning back. It is difficult to doubt God. I wonder if that was how Moses was able to circle the impossible promise of meat to eat. God had already sent manna. God had already parted the Red Sea. God had already performed ten miraculous signs and delivered Israel out of Egypt.

How can you *not* believe when God has proven Himself over and over again?

One footnote.

This question — Is there a limit to my power? — is translated differently in different versions of the Bible. One version reads, "Is the LORD's arm too short?" Another translation reads, "Is the LORD's hand waxed short?" In both instances, the hand or arm of the Lord is referenced as a metaphor for God's power.

With this as a backdrop, reconsider the ten miracles God performed to deliver Israel out of Egypt. These miracles are not attributed to the hand of God or arm of God.

"This is the finger of God."

While we don't know which finger it was, those ten miracles were attributed to one digit. My guess? His pinky! And if one finger is capable of ten miracles, then what can the hand of God or arm of God accomplish?

When it comes to the will of God, I'm hit-and-miss. And my prayer batting average is no better than anyone else when it comes to hitting God's curveballs. I often second-guess the will of God, but I don't doubt the power of God. God is able. I don't always know if He will, but I always know that He can.

15.5 Billion Light-Years

While God's power is technically measureless, the prophet Isaiah gives us a glimpse of God's omnipotence and omniscience by comparing them to the size of the universe. The distance between His wisdom and ours, His power and ours, is likened to the distance from one side of the universe to the other.

> "As the heavens are higher than
>   the earth,
>   so are my ways higher than
>   your ways
>   and my thoughts than your
>   thoughts."

The universe is so large that it requires an awfully long tape measure. The basic unit of measurement is a light-year. Light travels at 186,000 miles per second, which is so fast that in the time it takes to snap your fingers, light circumnavigates the globe half a dozen times.

To put the speed of light and size of the universe into perspective, the sun is 94.4 million miles away from the earth at its farthest distance from us. If you could drive to the sun traveling 65 miles per hour, 24 hours a day, 365 days a year, it would take you more than 163 years to get there. The light that warms your face on a sunny day, on the other hand, left the surface of the sun only 8 minutes ago. So while 94.4 million miles may seem like a long distance by earthly standards, it's our next-door neighbor by celestial measurements. The sun is the nearest star in our tiny little galaxy known as the Milky Way. There are more than 80 billion galaxies in the universe, which, for the record, equates to more than 10 galaxies per person! I don't think you have to worry about running out of things to do when you get to heaven. It's an awfully big sandbox.

In one minute, light travels 11 million miles. In one day, light travels 160 billion miles. In one year, light travels an unfathomable 5 trillion, 865 billion, 696 million miles. But that's just one light-year. The outer edge of the universe, according to astrophysicists, is 15.5 billion light-years away! If that seems incomprehensible, it's because it's virtually unimaginable. Yet God says that this is the distance between His thoughts and our thoughts. So here's my thought: Your best thought on your best day falls 15.5 billion light-years short of how great and how good God really is. Even the most brilliant among us underestimate God by 15.5 billion light-years. God is able to do 15.5 billion light-years beyond what you can ask or imagine.

By definition, a big dream is a dream that is bigger than you. In other words, it's beyond your human ability to accomplish. And this means there will be moments when you doubt yourself. That's normal. But that's when you need to remind yourself that your dream isn't bigger than God; God is 15.5 billion light-years bigger than your dream.

If you've never had a God-sized dream that scared you half to death, then you haven't really come to life. If you've never been overwhelmed by the impossibility of your plans, then your God is too small. If your vision isn't perplexingly impossible, then you need to expand the radiuses of your prayer circles.

Qualified Versus Called

A big dream is simultaneously the best feeling and worst feeling in the world. It's exhilarating because it's beyond your ability; it's frightening for the same exact reason. So if you are going to dream big, you have to manage the emotional tension. Facing your fears is the beginning of the battle. Then you have to circle them over and over again.

Have you ever felt like your dream was too big for you?

Moses felt that way more than once. When God called him to lead the Israelites out of Egypt, Moses felt like it was too big. He felt like he wasn't qualified, so he asked God to send someone else to do it. That is par for the course. In my experience, you'll never feel qualified. But God doesn't call the qualified; God qualifies the called.

I wasn't qualified to pastor National Community Church. The only thing I had on my résumé was a nine-week summer internship. We had no business going into the coffeehouse business. No one on our team had ever worked in a coffeehouse when we started pursuing that dream. But it doesn't matter if you qualify for the loan, qualify for the job, or qualify for the program. If God has called you, you're qualified.

The issue is never, "Are you qualified?" The issue is always, "Are you called?"

I make this distinction between *qualified* and *called* with aspiring writers all the time. Too many authors worry about whether or not their book will get published. That isn't the question.

The Circle Maker Participant's Guide with DVD

Trusting God with
Your Biggest Dreams
and Greatest Fears

Mark Batterson

This four-session video-based study helps participants gain a deeper understanding of prayer and, in turn, make a more consistent practice of prayer. It will give viewers new vocabulary and methodology to pray with a holy confidence and will help them dream big, pray hard, and think long. The video sessions combine teaching elements with creative elements to draw viewers into the circle. Pack includes one softcover participant's guide and one DVD.

Session Titles:
The Legend of the Circle Maker
The 1st Circle: Dream Big
The 2nd Circle: Pray Hard
The 3rd Circle: Think Long

Also available: Curriculum Kit

*Available in stores
and online January 2012!*

The Circle Maker

Praying Circles
Around Your
Biggest Dreams and
Greatest Fears

Mark Batterson

According to Pastor Mark
Batterson, "Drawing prayer
circles around our dreams isn't just a mechanism
whereby we accomplish great things for God. It's
a mechanism whereby God accomplishes great
things in us."

Do you ever sense that there is far more to
prayer and to God's vision for your life than
what you're experiencing? It's time you learned
from the legend of Honi the circle maker — a man
bold enough to draw a circle in the sand and not
budge from inside it until God answered his
prayers for his people.

What impossibly big dream is God calling you
to draw a prayer circle around? Sharing inspir-
ing stories from his own experiences as a circle
maker, Mark Batterson will help you uncover
your heart's deepest desires and God-given
dreams and unleash them through the kind of
audacious prayer that God delights to answer.

*Available in stores
and online January 2012!*

The Circle Maker Participant's Guide with DVD

Trusting God with Your Biggest Dreams and Greatest Fears

Mark Batterson

This four-session video-based study helps participants gain a deeper understanding of prayer and, in turn, make a more consistent practice of prayer. It will give viewers new vocabulary and methodology to pray with a holy confidence and will help them dream big, pray hard, and think long. The video sessions combine teaching elements with creative elements to draw viewers into the circle. Pack includes one softcover participant's guide and one DVD.

Session Titles:
The Legend of the Circle Maker
The 1st Circle: Dream Big
The 2nd Circle: Pray Hard
The 3rd Circle: Think Long

Also available: Curriculum Kit

*Available in stores
and online January 2012!*

Find Mark online at www.markbatterson.com,
on Facebook at www.facebook.com/markbatterson,
and on Twitter @MarkBatterson.

Share Your Thoughts

With the Author: Your comments will be forwarded to
the author when you send them to *zauthor@zondervan.com*.

With Zondervan: Submit your review of this book
by writing to *zreview@zondervan.com*.

Free Online Resources at
www.zondervan.com

Zondervan AuthorTracker: Be notified whenever your favorite
authors publish new books, go on tour, or post an update
about what's happening in their lives at www.zondervan.com/
authortracker.

Daily Bible Verses and Devotions: Enrich your life with daily
Bible verses or devotions that help you start every morning
focused on God. Visit www.zondervan.com/newsletters.

Free Email Publications: Sign up for newsletters on Christian
living, academic resources, church ministry, fiction, children's
resources, and more. Visit www.zondervan.com/newsletters.

Zondervan Bible Search: Find and compare Bible passages in
a variety of translations at www.zondervanbiblesearch.com.

Other Benefits: Register to receive online benefits like
coupons and special offers, or to participate in research.

ZONDERVAN®

ZONDERVAN.com/
AUTHORTRACKER
follow your favorite authors